I0004552

Blockchain

Easiest Ultimate Guide To Understand Blockchain

By

Jared Norton

© **Copyright 2016 Jared Norton - All rights reserved.**

This document is geared towards providing exact and reliable information in regards to the topic and issue covered. The publication is sold with the idea that the publisher is not required to render accounting, officially permitted, or otherwise, qualified services. If advice is necessary, legal or professional, a practiced individual in the profession should be ordered.

- From a Declaration of Principles which was accepted and approved equally by a Committee of the American Bar Association and a Committee of Publishers and Associations.

In no way is it legal to reproduce, duplicate, or transmit any part of this document in either electronic means or in printed format. Recording of this publication is strictly prohibited and any storage of this document is not allowed unless with written permission from the publisher. All rights reserved.

The information provided herein is stated to be truthful and consistent, in that any liability, in terms of inattention or otherwise, by any usage or abuse of any policies, processes, or directions contained within is the solitary and utter responsibility of the recipient reader. Under no circumstances will any legal responsibility or blame be held against the publisher for any reparation, damages, or monetary loss due to the information herein, either directly or indirectly.

Respective authors own all copyrights not held by the publisher.

The information herein is offered for informational purposes solely, and is universal as so. The presentation of the information is without contract or any type of guarantee assurance.

The trademarks that are used are without any consent, and the publication of the trademark is without permission or backing by the trademark owner. All trademarks and brands within this book are for clarifying purposes only and are the owned by the owners themselves, not affiliated with this document.

Table of Contents

Introduction

Nobody likes banks and, for a lot of people, it's for good reason. You go to the teller window five minutes before closing time and she won't acknowledge you because she just wants to close up and go home. Your Paypal account is tied to the banking system and they may yank your account access simply because you got an unusually large payment for something you sold on eBay. You wonder if the homeless aren't caught in some kind of Catch-22 where they can't get access to a decent apartment without a bank account and can't get a bank account without a photo ID that includes their home address.

All of these are good points that could be solved with a new digital currency called Bitcoin. Bitcoin is always open for business and won't ignore you even when you want to use it to have a pizza delivered at two in the morning. It won't shut you out simply because you received a transaction worth thousands of dollars from someone buying your car. If you want to use it, literally all you need to do is download the wallet on a laptop or tablet.

That wallet is the app that enables you to access the Bitcoin network that includes nodes on which transaction data is stored and processors that, obviously, process transactions. If you simply want to earn Bitcoin and spend Bitcoin, downloading the wallet on a device that is capable of handling it is all you need to do – no photo ID or home address required.

Bitcoin users like it for a wide variety of reasons. It's relatively anonymous in the sense that their sensitive financial data won't be compromised if a retailer's credit card servers get hacked. Businesses like it because it's easy to integrate into a Point-of-Sale system, it protects the vendor against fraudulent chargebacks, and they don't have to pay the high fees that credit cards charge for payment processing when somebody pays with Bitcoin. Freelancers like it because it's an easy way to get paid across international borders even when Paypal won't operate in their home country. It's easy to track down the details of any transaction if there's any question about what happened.

This is made possible by technology that doesn't care about much of anything except whether you have a device that can link to the Internet even if it means soaking up the free Wi-Fi at the coffee shop and the ability to copy-and-paste a string of letters and numbers or scan a QR code. It's called the Blockchain, a decentralized ledger that keeps track of debits and credits for all Bitcoin users.

There are many ways that the Blockchain can benefit entrepreneurs beyond the fact that it's associated with a currency that makes fraudulent chargebacks impossible. It can be used for many applications that require a reliable and tamper-resistant means of record-keeping. It can be used to give you a competitive edge in a world where the economy is becoming increasingly global and customers increasingly care about how their goods are produced and can hop from one "next big thing" to the next pretty fast. If you're looking at the Blockchain, you probably have a few questions.

What's The Blockchain?

Bitcoin is seen as the advent of an innovative new currency for the digital world. However, an associated technology called the Blockchain has been getting more attention lately. The first question usually is, "What is the Blockchain, anyway?"

The simplest answer is that the Blockchain is a secure, transparent and decentralized ledger. "Secure" doesn't mean that it tries to hide information. It simply means that nobody's going to tamper with records on the Blockchain without sending up red flags that would be very quickly noticed by alert Blockchain developers. Even if somebody does attempt to fraudulently alter records, the original records will still exist on the valid Blockchain and can be pinned down by comparing information on duplicate records.

The Blockchain is designed to use a cryptographic hash and timestamps to make its records unalterable once they are created. This makes it possible for Blockchain experts to inspect records on the Blockchain to determine the facts of any given transaction or to detect attempts to tamper with the ledger. As we saw with the swift reaction to a faulty update in 2013, an accidental technical glitch that affects the Blockchain's ability to create reliable records can be quickly isolated and shut down. The same principles that made that possible also provides a reliable way to detect and isolate a deliberate attempt to tamper with records before it goes too far.

Bitcoin's decentralized Blockchain ledger ensures that no party in a transaction will have to trust any single third party to essentially hold their money for them. While the technology behind the Blockchain can be used to create an effective automated escrow system, the basic system is not going to disappear with your money or deny you access to your account. That gives Bitcoin its power as a currency that can cross international borders, provide quick settlements and avoid being controlled by any centralized authority.

Maintaining the Blockchain relies on the operation of multiple nodes that are capable of storing transaction data and the operation of processors that can validate new data. Think of the nodes as completely equal servers that regularly update one another with data and make it possible for authenticated clients to connect to them, if you like. The multiple, regularly updated nodes builds in a considerable amount of redundancy into the system. If a node malfunctions, the IT staff can work with a Blockchain expert to isolate the server and troubleshoot that node to determine what went wrong. Common malfunctions will usually involve a node's failure to transmit valid records. It may transmit records that make no sense to other nodes. It may refuse to transmit any sort of data at all. It might "go rogue," create its own version of the Blockchain and create records that the other nodes cannot use in any meaningful way. In cases like this, an alert Blockchain expert will ask the IT staff to isolate the server from the rest of the network until he can pin down and fix the problem.

If a node malfunctions and has to be isolated for maintenance in a business that relies on access to real-time data, the result is not wasted time and loss of revenues when the business also makes use of Blockchain applications. The result is that the remaining nodes pick up the slack and clients can quickly reconnect to a working node. That's good for a business owner who doesn't want to explain to frustrated clients why a server in a centralized network is down.

The Blockchain was originally designed to be a decentralized system that keeps track of debits and credits. The existence of thousands of

Bitcoin nodes on six continents demonstrates the Blockchains capacity to become effectively the "World Wide Web" of finance. A private version of the Blockchain can work if each branch of a business with multiple locations is willing to run a node that clients can connect to.

What Makes The Blockchain Secure?

The original version of the Blockchain makes use of a cryptographic hash known as SHA-256. It's secure, but so inefficient that specialized hardware called mining rigs has been created specifically to handle the job of processing transactions. These mining rigs solve mathematical problems called hashes to confirm and relay valid transactions.

Each solved hash represents one block – a bundle of processed transactions that can be relayed to all valid nodes. The cryptographic information on each block of records is based on the information associated with the last block and contains a unique timestamp, which makes visualizations of the Blockchain look like links in a chain. In fact, the term "Blockchain" comes from the idea that it's a cryptographically secured chain of record blocks.

This chain of blocks makes it easy to detect attempts to fraudulently add records to the chain. Imagine that you're adding links to a chain and someone comes along, chooses a link in the middle of the chain and starts adding his own links to that link. The chain has just been forked. The Blockchain can be similarly forked and actually was forked by that faulty update in 2013, but the swift reaction by Bitcoin developers shows that it's possible to quickly recognize and isolate a fraudulent fork if it happens.

Why would somebody fraudulently fork a Blockchain? They might do it because they want to falsely edit a record that already exist on the chain, so they fork the chain just before the block that contains that record. This may become a common tactic with anyone who wishes to fraudulently alter a contract, deed or title if attempts to fork the chain are not detected and censored too quickly to make such an attempt worth the effort and risk.

They may fork a Blockchain because they wish to take control of the system altogether. By default, the version of the chain that can command more processing power and, thus, create the longer chain of blocks is regarded as the valid one. Bitcoin regularly sets world records with the amount of processing power it commands, so most people would consider an attack on Bitcoin to be more expensive than it's worth, but most Blockchain networks just don't command that much processing power. Somebody who wants to take over an abandoned cryptocurrency wouldn't even have to fork it at all. He could just set up a node or two and a few modest mining rigs to work on validating new records as part of the process of rebooting it. (Of course, that would be the EASY part when it comes to rebooting a currency that has been abandoned by its original developers.)

In both cases, it's simple enough to compare the cryptographic hash and timestamp of the records in question to determine which is the original, valid record. The accidental 2013 fork was resolved by warning miners to not switch over to the "new" version of the Bitcoin Blockchain. Although the Blockchain is designed to be secure, this also demonstrates the value of having alert experts and developers on the scene in case a fork happens.

An alert Blockchain expert can isolate a node that is malfunctioning or showing signs of tampering and investigate the matter. Maybe the node is spewing fake and/or nonsensical records. Maybe the node isn't relaying new records at all. Maybe the node has created its own little version of the Blockchain and that's when the Blockchain expert is really going to start asking the tough questions. Why is it forked, and what kind of funny business is the branch manager involved in now?

This is actually one of the benefits of having a decentralized system that can handle multiple nodes in more than one location. It's easy to isolate a "rogue" node for troubleshooting without compromising the rest of the system. The behaving nodes can just keep plugging away, creating new valid records and making them available for anyone who wants to inspect or use them, while the Blockchain expert investigates what went wrong with the misbehaving node. Then, once the matter is settled, the fork can be resolved and the repaired node can be added to the network again.

What Can The Blockchain Be Used For?

Think of the Blockchain as a technology that could enable the "Internet of Finances," if you like. We already have a worldwide financial system, but it's an inefficient one with unnecessary built-in costs for its users. Think of it as a train that loses a lot of its kinetic energy to friction and heat, if you like. It could probably operate more efficiently if the track was kept in good repair and it's designed to run more effectively on that track. The Blockchain and the network it runs on can provide the more efficient track if we can build the better train.

The Blockchain can be used for not only keeping track of debits and credits for a currency system like Bitcoin, but also for keeping track of any data that might involve a transaction or record of ownership in some way. Estonia is already using the Blockchain in an effort to clean up its notary system. If you've ever dealt with a notary service in some way, you may have wondered how notary agents know that their clients aren't committing fraud. The real truth is that notary agents can be distracted, fooled or bribed into enabling fraud and this exact issue is the reason that Estonia teamed up with BitNation to unravel fraudulent tactics on the part of the notary public.

Even the Internet of Things could become involved when a Blockchain-enabled smart lock denies access to a tenant who failed to pay the rent or a Smart Car drives itself back to the dealership because the owner has been missing payments. This is actually a benefit of using a system that is completely neutral. Once you've signed the contract, it's assumed that you knew precisely what you were agreeing to. If you wake up and your garage is empty because you missed payments on your car loan, at least you're going to know where you car is at. On the flip side, the

Blockchain protects your rights, too, by automating the process of logging payments. You can make your monthly payments by sending some form of cryptocurrency to a unique address that is monitored by the Smart Contract. The car is not going to drive itself back to the dealership because the banker forgot to log a payment.

Nobody who knows quality sunglasses pretty well is going to think that you can get authentic Ray-Bans for $10. For more important things, the Blockchain can keep track of where supplies come from. Existing Blockchain supply chain apps include Provenance, which works with businesses to guarantee that products ranging from fish and seafood to backpacks come from legitimate sources. Greater transparency in the supply chain is the kind of thing that can earn consumers' trust in a world where people are becoming increasingly aware of issues such as the illegal or unsustainable harvesting of seafood or exploitive labor practices being used to produce products like backpacks. The Blockchain can provide that transparency when used to build a supply chain app that can guarantee the authenticity of products by rejecting any shipment that did not come from a recognized source.

A workflow app can work in a way that's similar to the supply chain to point out places where processes that are important to your business are getting bottlenecked. Sometimes a location or department just isn't being as productive as it could be. The problem might even be a third party vendor that isn't delivering the quality service you expected. An internal application that adds functionality to what Trello can already do can eliminate the perception that you just have to put up with whatever is causing the bottleneck. With a Blockchain workflow app, you get unalterable documentation that you can stand on when you eliminate the cause of the bottleneck.

Reputation is very important to a business. Businesses will literally pay money to third party review sites to hide negative reviews, pay hack writers to post glowing reviews of their own business or attack a competitor with negative reviews, or give free products to professional reviewers in exchange for an "honest" review. What a Blockchain reputation app can do more reliably is act as a sidechain for a Smart Contract app that can read records on the contract chain but not create new records. This reputation app can keep track of how many times that interested parties have reneged on a contract or triggered clauses on their contract that caused a refund to be issued. Did an Internet service provider throttle the Internet access for its users? Not only will those users get a refund from the Smart Contracts involved, but the reputation sidechain will register that as a ding to the ISP's reputation. Businesses that work together to maintain a Smart Contract system with attached reputation sidechain can gain a competitive advantage even over businesses that are members of the Better Business Bureau simply because it feels less like a simple "good old boys' club" for businesses. Rather, it feels like one that is less vulnerable to "negative review attack" by a competitor because its job is to keep track of the numbers that represent a business's actual performance.

This works because the Blockchain is transparent enough to make information stored on it easy to search and read. It won't even make you jump through hoops, create an account or sign up for an email newsletter to get the information you want. If you are looking for information about a Bitcoin payment and have the transaction ID, an IP address or one of the Blockchain addresses involved in the transaction, it's easy enough to search on Blockchain.info for that information.

This kind of transparency can be combined with the fact that you aren't storing your customers' credit card information when they pay with cryptocurrencies to reassure them that you care enough to earn their trust. They can type your business name into a search app and find everything they want to know about your business' track record. It provides the raw numbers in a way that's easy to read. How many times have you taken a contract to a successful conclusion? Does the customer service seem to decline steadily once you've made the sale, leading to a lot of customers canceling contracts on their own? As with the workflow app, the right kind of reputation app can point you to the one location or element that might be causing problems for an otherwise good business.

So if it requires a reliable and transparent way to keep records, the Blockchain can be used as a base to build an app for that. That transparency can reassure consumers that the vendor is being honest or help them avoid dishonest vendors. The Blockchain also protects the rights of both consumers and vendors by recording the details of any given transaction, contract or document on the notary system in a way that is difficult to dispute.

How Inclusive Is The Blockchain?

Modern Western society cares about including as many people as possible in its socioeconomic system, but the centralized financial system hasn't gotten the memo yet. Two billion humans do not have convenient or cheap access to banking services. What makes the Blockchain different is that it can be as inclusive as you like.

It does not matter to the Blockchain if you have no assets and no photo ID card when you download a client. The Bitcoin wallet is a client that connects to nodes on the Bitcoin network. Bitcoin is more inclusive than banks because you don't have to establish much of anything except your ability to actually use that client. That's something that ought to make cryptocurrencies popular with the homeless who don't have a street address but do have a cheap laptop that works.

To the Blockchain, fairness is the ability to use its system on an equal footing with every other user. If you are a freelancer, you might bid on jobs on sites like XBTFreelancer along with every other freelancer who is interested in making a Bitcoin. If you have some used items that you want to sell but don't want to use eBay, you might try Bitify. You might even have some luck with buying and selling on the Bitcointalk Marketplace if you can put up with having to establish yourself as part of the Bitcoin community first. The point here is that Blockchain applications like Bitcoin are remarkably easy to start using within minutes of downloading the client no matter who you are.

This is true even in countries where Paypal doesn't operate and the use of credit cards is not commonplace. Many participants in some countries' marketplaces prefer to use cash or the digital equivalent of cash because it's just more convenient than going to the bank. Kenya's

MPesa is a success for exactly this reason. If an entrepreneur is considering expanding operations into one of these countries or even just hiring the occasional freelancer who resides in an area where Paypal won't work, this is something that will have to be accounted for. From the perspective of someone living in one of these countries, if he can't pay or be paid with a currency like MPesa or Bitcoin or a few paper bills in his native currency, he's not going to see the use of participating. So using Bitcoin and the Blockchain can easily help you, as an entrepreneur, participate in the worldwide market.

Even if you prefer not to make your identity known (and nobody ever did reliably confirm Bitcoin creator Satoshi Nakamoto's real identity), Bitcoin makes it possible to do business anywhere at any time. Bitcoin crosses international borders easily, which makes it increasingly popular for Filipinos working abroad who want to send money home to their families in the Philippines. In its pure form, Bitcoin is cheap, fast, secure, and will get your money into the hands of the recipients while rarely, if ever, being touched by third parties who will inevitably want their slice of the pie.

The Blockchain can do the same thing because, well, it was introduced as part of the Bitcoin package. Bitcoin gambling sites use the term "provably fair" to show that their algorithms have not been unfairly weighted against its players even when the odds are already against them. Dice games are hard enough to win even when the dice aren't loaded. Entities that are interested in using the Blockchain should adapt the concept of "provably fair" to ensure that everybody can participate in voluntary transactions without the deck being stacked in the house's favor even when they start with nothing and the odds are already against them.

That means there should be no artificial barriers to access, no entry fees (beyond, obviously, obtaining a mobile device that's capable of running the Blockchain client of your choice), and a friendly environment for businesses who are willing to take the risks involved in transacting with people they might never know the names of. I can buy pizza with a few hundredths of a Bitcoin and they never need to record my name or financial information in any permanent form. People respond better if they can do the equivalent of buying pizza – paying for results without having to pay in advance or show an ID – simply because they may not have the money in hand to pay an up-front fee or a photo ID that proves that they are who they say they are.

The Human Element

Reasonable Blockchain supporters don't try to pretend that the human element won't ever be a factor. When the Bitcoin Blockchain was accidentally forked in 2013, the humans on the Bitcoin development team detected the problem, investigated and warned owners of mining rigs to not switch over to the faulty update that caused the fork. By admitting that the update was not functioning as intended and fixing the problem quickly, they earned the trust of the Bitcoin community.

There will be times when you'll need an equally alert person watching the Blockchain apps for signs of a possible malfunction. When your business has grown to the point where you have eight locations in five cities, you'll naturally want to have a node at each location, but how do you make sure that a dishonest location manager won't try to tamper with a node in an attempt to make himself look more effective than he really is? Ideally, such a thing would be easy to deal with, especially when that node forks the chain multiple times and always seems to do so in a way that makes the manager look good. Just make sure that the Blockchain expert on your IT staff stays on top of it while you deal with the dishonest manager.

Blockchain apps are good at generating and storing data in a reliable way, but have limited ability to make decisions beyond what they're programmed to do. This means you might miss opportunities if you rely too much on the automated nature of the Blockchain. Where can you find a better price on office supplies? Should you reinstate a contract that was deactivated because the client was late on the monthly payments for three months in a row? Should you buy that stock that has plummeted in value recently but otherwise has a history of performing well? These are questions that a Blockchain app might not be able to answer because it's not programmed to look for the appropriate indicators.

The Blockchain is a way to process and store records in a way that the humans viewing it can trust. It can't make the kind of decision that requires intuition or an ability to jump on an opportunity that your automated stock trading software might miss. Look at it this way: How many times have you wished you could have gone back in time and invested in Bitcoin when it was still worth five cents? The data makes it possible to spot trends early, but one common saying about trends is that, if you can spot it, the trend is already almost over. It's up to you to decide whether to buy, hold, sell, or invest in that innovative new technology instead.

That doesn't mean you have to obsess about watching the data scroll that represents new Bitcoin transactions on Blockchain.info. It just means that it never hurts to check and use your intuition when a new opportunity comes to light. It means you should stay alert and be ready to jump on opportunities that your applications might miss.

The Blockchain As Part Of Future Economics

Most entrepreneurs don't think much about what the economic climate will look like centuries from now. They're thinking about how their business can get through the next month, quarter, and year. However, highly successful entrepreneurs usually have a long-term plan that will get them through the next ten years. The quarterly report matters, but so does making sure the business will still be relevant when consumers move on to the next big thing.

For this reason, it pays to implement the tools that a savvy entrepreneur needs to stay flexible. Consumers are becoming increasingly concerned about where the products they buy every day come from, so a Blockchain supply chain app can reassure them that the products you sell come from ethical and sustainable sources along with enabling you to avoid fraud at any point in the supply chain. An internal workflow app can give you a clear picture of how smoothly operations are proceeding within your business and react more quickly to places where the workflow is getting bottlenecked. As importantly for your business, the Blockchain can enable you to compete on an international playing field by making it possible to attract international customers with a reduced reliance on international third party financial institutions.

At this point, the Blockchain could be called a bandwagon, but it's not one that's out of control and is going to crash. The commonly used selling points used by Bitcoin supporters are that it's cheap, fast, secure, and protects the rights of the recipient. When you do a lot of international business, the Bitcoin that international customers send to you will usually be in your wallet in an hour, tops. When you send money to an international contractor, he'll like that he doesn't have to wait days to get his money like he would if you use Western Union or Paypal. Bitcoin will even work in nations that Paypal doesn't, so you'll never even have to wonder if your contractor got his money as long as you sent it to the right Bitcoin address. Blockchain applications can use the same properties that make it easy for Bitcoin to leap over international borders to protect the interests of all parties in a transaction regardless of where they are in the world.

This makes the Blockchain useful for an economy that is increasingly global. If you live in the U.S., you could easily hire a French freelancer to translate some text from American English to French to use on the French-language version of your website. He may insist on being paid in X amount of Bitcoin simply because it's easier than worrying about currency exchange rates. That same freelancer could then use that Bitcoin to pay for his personal expenses even if he doesn't have a bank account. He can literally use Bitcoin to buy a pizza and the pizza place doesn't even need to know his name, much less his financial information.

Which brings us to the next interesting point about what the Blockchain could enable for the future of economics. International organizations have estimated that as many as two billion people cannot conveniently access the financial services that the rest of us take for granted. They may have to walk for two days to get to a bank. They might not be able to open a bank account. Banks may charge high fees for the "convenience" of cashing a paycheck if the holder of that check does not have an account. Most of these people give up on the idea of buying and selling on an equal footing with the rest of us simply because the banks treat them unfairly.

However, Blockchain applications and cryptocurrencies like Bitcoin can include these people. Unlike banks, Bitcoin does not care if you have no assets. A Blockchain Smart Contract application would only say something to the effect of, "Sign here, and don't forget to make your payments or turn in your work on time," without requiring proof of identity. The same hands that weave a basket can also log that basket on a Blockchain supply chain application used by retailers that sell Fair Trade products.

When a national economic system includes more laborers that can sell their labor on the open market for a fair price, one of the first things that nation notices is a sharp increase in its GDP. This happens because more people are buying and selling on an equal footing. That nation might have seen a recent influx of honest and hardworking immigrants or it may have recently had a successful civil rights campaign that convinced the local elite of the value of including previously marginalized groups in its mainstream economic system. An increase in population alone does not always equal any significant jump in value produced *per capita*, but an increase of an area's population that is actively buying and selling goods and services on the open market does.

The same can be true in a Blockchain-based economic system in which nobody has to show a valid photo ID card or be able to verify a Paypal account in order to buy and sell on the international market. When these two billion unbanked people have access to cryptocurrency and Blockchain clients, you can hire them to take care of those tasks that aren't really worth hiring a permanent employee for but need to be done anyway, and they can use those cryptocurrencies to buy the goods and services they need. This is a matter of practical economics and not just platitudes. When more people are included in a socioeconomic system and can buy and sell in a truly free market, it enriches everybody because it produces more value per capita.

This matters for the same reason that professional football players rarely complain even when they lose if they know that the playing field was level, the balls weren't deflated by a cheater on the other team, and the referees did not obviously favor one team over the other. A truly free market that includes technologies like the Blockchain sets things up so that there is no centralized authority that can choose winners and losers. It just makes sure everybody gets a chance to play.

For these reasons, the Blockchain could be called a truly 21st century financial technology that can solve the inefficiencies of an international financial system that hasn't gotten the memo yet. The idea of an economic future that includes decentralized fintech is good for you as a small business owner who maybe isn't ready to compete on the international market, but wouldn't mind hiring an international freelancer to handle a one-off job every once in a while. That's also good for the unbanked who would genuinely have something to offer if only they could participate in the worldwide marketplace on a more even footing. That's the kind of economic future the Blockchain could enable.

Cryptocurrencies And The Blockchain As Part Of A Marketing Drive

Do you remember the Bitcoin Bowl? I won't be very surprised if you don't. BitPay sponsored the St. Petersburg Bowl for one year, but then pulled out because it wasn't as successful as BitPay had hoped. If anything, it gave football fans who attended the St. Petersburg Bowl a chance to use Bitcoin to pay for concessions and souvenirs at the stadium.

However, entrepreneurs can use cryptocurrencies and the Blockchain as a more successful way to market their businesses. Install a Bitcoin ATM and run a promotion. "Triple points on your rewards card if you buy with Bitcoin!" Hand out a fact sheet explaining what Bitcoin is. When customers get used to the idea of paying for their purchases using this Internet funny money that so recently topped $600 in value, that's when you can start introducing the concept of using Blockchain apps as part of everyday business.

Education is important here. At this point, they probably don't care what kind of ledger you use as long as you aren't fudging the numbers too much. However, they do care that they won't be charged an early cancellation fee at a membership gym because a dishonest manager changed the signing date on their contract. It has been known to happen and customers are very sensitive about fraud on that level. They need to know that your business and its employees are never going to be given a chance to stoop that low. They like to know that they can trust you no matter what kind of business you run. So educating them about what the Blockchain can do for them can become a very effective part of a marketing drive.

You may have seen those videos that were basically an introduction to Bitcoin 101. They can explain Bitcoin in plain English to people who've never heard of it, except maybe in the newspapers, and they think it's this weird Internet funny money that seems to go hand in hand with the Dark Web. You can show them otherwise by running your own series of videos that explains that not only can Bitcoin and the Blockchain be used for legitimate purposes, but they can also be used to ensure that customers are dealing with completely honest and aboveboard businesses like yours.

"If our Internet service ever drops below the speed that we guaranteed, our Blockchain-based contract management system will automatically issue a credit on your bill or give you a refund."

"We track our sources of seafood on a completely transparent Blockchain supply chain system so that you can see where your seafood purchases are coming from."

This is the kind of thing that can hook customers that are going to be around for the long haul. The gecko is cute, but "15 minutes can save you 15% on your car insurance" is what gets people to check out the Geico website. It's information that the customer can use wrapped up in a format that's easy to remember even when the customer doesn't take action right away. If you can do something similar for the Blockchain, it tells people that you're using a new kind of technology that can benefit them as much as it benefits you.

Customers are pretty smart these days. They don't fall for the jingle. Instead, they want to know what makes you different from all of your competitors. That's why you should work the Blockchain apps you decide to use into your marketing campaign.

The Blockchain For Your Bottom Line

The bottom line here is that the Blockchain is good for your bottom line if you care about staying flexible enough to stay relevant. As we've seen with fads like Beanie Babies and Pokemon, these things can come and go before you can even blink and you want to make use of technologies that actually have some staying power even when today's hot sellers become tomorrow's garage sale offerings. The Blockchain could have that staying power among international businesses simply because it can make financial dealings much more efficient without even worrying about what the foreign exchange is going to do very much. It's assumed that a Bitcoin is a Bitcoin regardless of whether you spend it in the U.S., France, or Japan.

With Blockchain technology, you can send money to or receive money from anywhere on Earth cheaply and quickly. You can form contracts with anyone, anywhere, at any time, with very few worries about whether the other party is going to actually follow through. You can quickly size up the reputation of any party you're considering doing business with, track down any problems with your supply chain, and check the notary system to see who currently owns an asset. You can do all this with very few worries about a third party getting into the middle of a transaction and denying you permission to use what you own.

The Blockchain can handle all this because it's designed to store data in a transparent, foolproof and cryptographically secured way. Bitcoin and Blockchain insiders like to use the term "trustless" to describe the idea that you technically don't have to trust a third party to use the technology. If you have the choice between taking a chance on a third party vendor and coming off as a control freak who insists that everything be done in-house, always be the control freak. That way, your customers know that you care about controlling as many factors as possible when they trust you with their information.

It might sound peculiar that using trustless technology in this way can lead to greater trust from your customers. However, if a third party vendor you trusted to store data is found to be violating data privacy regulations, you will usually be found liable for fines and possible compensation of customers for financial losses they suffered because you chose the wrong vendor. The argument that a third party vendor failed you is unlikely to impress your customers or a jury. So, if you can, hire an expert who can set up your Blockchain applications and install nodes at each of your locations for you.

The coolest part? You can actually use Bitcoin to pay for part of your business expenses instead of simply dumping it on the exchanges. Gyft and eGifter both sell electronic gift cards that can be used to buy office supplies, pay for your next business trip, pick up the tab at a dinner meeting, or do a giveaway as part of an inexpensive social media promotion. Next time you hire a freelancer or contractor, ask them if they accept Bitcoin. These days, it's increasingly likely that they'll say yes and send you their Bitcoin address, simply because they care about not waiting days to get their money after the job is done because Western Union and Paypal are taking their own sweet time. That's a good thing for you, especially if you can get the freelancer or contractor to digitally sign a Smart Contract as part of the process. Then cashing out becomes somebody else's problem while you use the Blockchain to keep your business running smoothly.

Does The Blockchain Have Any Weaknesses, Though?

The simple answer to this is: Not very many, if you implement the Blockchain as part as an overall Information Technology strategy. The Blockchain is a nearly foolproof way to process and store data, but may be susceptible to fraudulent actors running fake nodes, such as Chainalysis did in 2015 in what was called a partial Sybil attack. It was caught running fake nodes that clients could connect to, but these nodes were not relaying data to other nodes on the Bitcoin network. This is one of a few security concerns that users of Blockchain applications will have to watch out for.

Which means having a way to authenticate that the nodes connecting to your network are valid ones that are transmitting valid data and that the clients connecting to them are valid, as well. While Bitcoin users are accustomed to the idea that anyone with a cheap Android tablet can download a wallet, business owners will prefer a way to ensure that only authorized employees and devices can create new records. Your IT staff may be able to work together with Blockchain developers to create a "Blockchain Active Directory" that manages access privileges for both employees and customers.

For those who are not very familiar with Active Directory, it works by organizing users into groups and then assigning access privileges to certain resources to each group. The accounting department might have access to the monthly expense reports, but not the contracts with customers. Managers might have access to analyses of the workflow data so they can pin down bottlenecks. Customers may have the ability to view their contracts, get updates on the status of any orders they've placed, and request updates to their own information through a specialized client when appropriate. So Active Directory normally works by sorting access to resources by function.

It might even be a good idea to make use of semi-independent sidechains for each function. Very few Blockchain experts are going to recommend using just one Blockchain for all your important data because then you're running the risk of Blockchain bloat. This means that a Blockchain can require more storage capacity and more processing power than it absolutely has to because it's trying to store too much data. This obviously becomes a concern when you do not wish to store your accounting ledgers, contracts and workflow logs in the same database.

Instead, Blockchain developers will recommend using separate Blockchains that are often called *sidechains* because they can run parallel to one another, interacting only as necessary to serve their functions. This can speed up the process of creating new records and searching through existing records, as well as simplify the process of managing the Bitcoin Active Directory.

If keeping sensitive data from being stolen is a concern, you might hesitate to implement a technology that promises total transparency to anyone who is interested in inspecting records. On the one hand, such transparency can give you a competitive advantage with savvy consumers who care about doing business with someone who is trustworthy and uses responsible sourcing practices. On the other, a competitor might steal data from your R&D department and use that information to patent a possible future product before you can. That means managing the Blockchain's transparency wisely.

There are only a limited number of ways to counter the Blockchain's transparent nature except to implement a robust IT security protocol for servers on which the Blockchain applications are stored. However, Blockchains can be set up so that they don't interact with one another at all and might not even know that another Blockchain exists, applications can be implemented in a way that allows them to read data on a chain but not write data to that chain, and it's even possible for one Blockchain ledger to send "transactions" to another Blockchain ledger but not receive "transactions" from that other ledger in return.

Conclusion – Is The Blockchain Right For You?

Bitcoin is kind of hard to destroy. Disabling its network would require the destruction of the entire World Wide Web, and even then, there might still be a functional node in a bunker somewhere. Setting up your own Blockchain system can be as easy as hosting it on a server in your basement if your business is not yet at the point where you have multiple locations. If you can set up more than one server in multiple locations, this has the effect of automating the creation of backups in real-time and speeding up the process of recovering from a malfunction in one of the servers.

However, this should not be used as an excuse for ignoring the fact that customers trust you with your credit card information. The real truth is that being a small business should not be used as an excuse for ignoring security. Regulations regarding the storage of credit card information apply to you as much as it applies to large retailers like Target – who, as far as hackers were concerned, had a big fat target painted on its back in the form of millions of credit card numbers. Hackers are even increasingly targeting small businesses because they know that small business owners will often put off implementing appropriate security. There's just no workaround if you intend to accept credit card payments other than refusing to store that information any longer than you have to.

What it really boils down to is the trust issue. Customers trust you with their credit card information. They trust you to be an honest vendor of the products and services you provide. They trust you to make it right if things don't go as expected. One could argue that the Blockchain can take some of the headaches out of earning their repeat business. When it's stored in a way that can't be altered in any way, it makes it easier for all parties involved to point to what really happened, which makes it easier to resolve any issues.

This is an obvious reason to accept Bitcoin payments. While it probably won't replace credit cards among customers who care about convenience, you're taking advantage of the elements of Bitcoin that make it possible to accept payments without your customers' personal information being involved in the transaction. Then you can just log that the payment was received without associating their numbers with their names.

The Blockchain can help with management of your critical data when you care about making your IT staff look competent. Nobody's emails are going to just vanish and, even if an email server has a meltdown, the data will still be recoverable in cases where the hard drive didn't get shredded. The Blockchain provides decentralization, instant real-time backups, and an even lower risk of losing your valuable data to a hardware failure. If losing your valuable data like sensitive emails is going to lead to any kind of scandal and/or loss of trust, use the Blockchain and make sure all nodes stay up and running as much as possible.

Some industries have to deal with customers who are understandably nervous about fraud. Others have to deal with regulations that govern the handling of records. When implemented wisely, the use of technologies like the Blockchain can reassure customers and regulators that you're willing to go "above and beyond" to make certain that records are handled appropriately and can't be altered in any way once they've been added to the system.

It might sound weird that a trustless technology might help generate trust. However, the most important thing to remember about the Blockchain is that you don't necessarily have to trust a third party to even know what they're doing. You can just make sure you have all your important data pinned down on a few Blockchain apps and then just make sure you have somebody around who can ensure that everything is running smoothly. That way, you won't ever have to worry about things going wrong because your records got tampered with.

www.ingramcontent.com/pod-product-compliance
Lightning Source LLC
Chambersburg PA
CBHW070928050326
40689CB00015B/3658

9781537533377